JUST LIVE IT

Harriet Sleigh

RoperPenberthy Publishing Ltd
Horsham, England

Published by RoperPenberthy Publishing Ltd
PO Box 545, Horsham, England

First published in 2004

ISBN 1 903905 16 8

Cover design by Angie Moyler

Typeset by Avocet Typeset, Chilton, Aylesbury, Bucks
Printed in the United Kingdom by Bell & Bain Ltd, Scotland

FOREWORD

The life that Jesus Christ came to give us is not bland, boring or dry. It is full of vibrancy, excitement and joy. In other words, Jesus came so we might have genuine fullness of life. That life is like a seed within every born-again Christian. For a person to grow spiritually that life must be appropriated and lived out. A person is transformed by the growth of that life within them. It is not mere intellectual knowledge that transforms a person, it is the revelation of biblical truth by the Holy Spirit in a person's inner being that brings that new life out into the open. The crucifixion, death and resurrection of Jesus Christ have opened up for us a river of new life that is available to all. But we need to learn how to take hold and live in the good of what Jesus has made available to us. In my own life and ministry I have seen the transforming power of God operate through His Word and I know what riches lie in the pages of the bible. In these booklets, Harriet Sleigh provides invaluable tools for the Christian to grow in his or her spiritual life. The principles of scriptural meditation and confession are fundamental to appropriating the life contained in the bible. I encourage you to make full use of these materials and take hold of the abundant life that Jesus died to give you.

Colin Urquhart
October 2004

JUST LIVE IT

God wants to transform your life so it is not just an ordinary life, but an abundant life, one that overflows with good things. He made you; you are unique and He has a glorious purpose for you through which you will be truly fulfilled. This can only happen if you see it, want it, indeed, delight in it and then decide to go for God and His ways 100%. He knows exactly what you have been through. He was with you. He is going to use every experience good and bad, nothing will be wasted.

The speed with which you grow, that this abundant life becomes a reality, is dependent on three choices;

> **Choice 1)** a **decision** to say 'Yes' with all your heart; a passion to step into His glorious ways and be free from the old negative ways.
>
> **Choice 2)** a **decision** to receive whole-heartedly the Word of God, delighting to let it change you. This involves spending time with Him, and with the Word. The more time you spend, the more you are changed.
>
> **Choice 3)** a **decision** to live it, and you will discover that it works...

Before you were born again you may have tried to change certain things in your life, for example, to give up smoking, but found it hard, and often failed. Now you are born again, all is changed, because Jesus has already done it all for you when He died on the cross. The victory has already been won. You need to simply change the way you think of yourself, to let go your old negative way of thinking, and replace it with the glorious truths of who you are as described in the bible. You are **now** a new person. The old self-centred person you used to be, with all the bad habits, was crucified, and buried with Jesus. It no longer exists. When He arose from the dead with a new life, He gave that same life to you, – praise God. He has given you His nature, His love, peace, joy, wisdom and miracle working power. There is so much more. It is a glorious fact that you are no longer separate from Him. His very life flows through you. The bible describes your relation to Him as a branch is to a tree. His love, joy and authority can now flow through you as the sap of a tree flows through a branch.

The bible tell us, 'if anyone is in Christ, he is a new creation; old things have passed away; behold, all things, have become new'. He has totally changed us. A good illustration of this is the way a caterpillar changes into a glorious butterfly. It is the nature of caterpillars to crawl on their many legs. Life seems a struggle for them. Many are gobbled up by birds. Similarly our old self-centred lives were a struggle; fearful, protecting our self-image and pride, like being in a prison. It was our nature to easily get sick and depressed. Glory to God – Jesus has set us free. That caterpillar nature is dead, gone, passed away. We learn through the Word of God to live as new creations, as 'butterflies'. It is not the nature of 'butterflies', to be fearful or to get sick. 'Butterflies' learn how they can refuse to fear, refuse to be sick – praise God! As 'butterflies' we realize He has made us beautiful. It is natural for us to fly leaving all the negatives of the world on the ground below. God wants each one of us to live a supernatural life as Jesus did. 'As He is so are we in this world' (1 John 4: 17)

He has a glorious purpose for everyone of His children. There are no limitations to God. The bible speaks of David, who was the youngest child of a large, poor family, God made him King of His people. He used Moses when he was 80 years old to deliver God's people from slavery.

What God is looking for is not your background or your age, but your heart. If you decide with all your heart, with no compromise, to do whatever God calls you to do, you could be as David. He made mistakes, but God called him a man after His own heart.

HOW?

We discover it is through the power of the **Word of God**. The bible tells us that the Word is **living** (Heb 4: 12). What does this mean? As we receive it in our spirit, in our heart, as we think about it, as we delight in it, speak of it, and live it, we find – glory to God – that it works. We get to know the truth inside, deep within and the truth makes us free as we live it.

What follows are declarations from the scriptures that describe who I am **now**, my true identity, my new '**butterfly nature**'. They cover areas like;

How I am loved passionately by God

The awesome power of the cross – for example, I am free from
  my past

My new self or new identity – glory to God, I am a blessing

The authority that is now mine –so I can change circumstances

The day-to-day walk He expects of every believer – being aglow,
  burning in the spirit

His purposes, which are now part of me – to glorify our Lord

There are so many ways that the declarations can be used to receive
these glorious truths deep within. Speaking them out is effective. You
could speak out some or all of the truths each day. Spend a few days
delighting in a particular truth that touches your heart, feasting on the
scriptures; key ones are included. You will notice a change even after
one week. After a month it will be distinctive. After six months it will
be the natural way you see yourself. After that, God will continue to
reveal more and more of His secrets and mysteries; there is no limit,
these truths will take root deep within – wow! For as he thinks in his
heart so is he (Prov 23: 7).

He loves to open up the scriptures to each one of us so that they will
come alive, mean something specific to you in your present circumstances. I share some of the things He has said to me as I have read the
scriptures, (the words following the declarations which are in bold
print), so that you may be encouraged. Let Him whisper to you also
glorious aspects of the scripture you are feasting on. He longs to do
this for you and for you to walk in it – Glory to God!

This is followed by a short section called 'How to live a scripture',
which will show you how you can digest and live a particular scripture
which has impacted you – hallelujah.

MY TRUE IDENTITY

John 3: 3 – Most assuredly, I say to you, unless one is born again, he cannot see the kingdom of God (John 3.3).

This applies to everyone, whether living on the streets or in a mansion, illiterate or the most learned. No matter how educated we may be, we need to be born again. God made us in His image. He made us to know Him and through this to live a blessed abundant life. Deep within each one of us is our real heart, or spirit that longs to know God. Through our education we build up many barriers, ideas about ourselves of who we want to be or think we are. We may be very successful in worldly terms, yet inside we know there is more to life. Religion has focused on aspects of ourselves like our past, our qualities, our problems, which infact draw attention to our old 'caterpillar' selves and away from God. He wants to go straight to our heart and meet us there. Glory to God, when we respond, we find that the other problems, the self issues, melt away as we come to know that Almighty God loves us, and longs to do glorious things in and through our lives.

Many know about God, but do you know God, know of His love for you? If not, or you are not sure, right now decide this is for me. It is only when you are born again that your eyes are open and you are able to see and step into the glorious truths. Be sure you have responded from your heart to His invitation and receive His life.

'For God so loved the world that He gave His only begotten Son, that whoever believes in Him should not perish but have everlasting life.' John 3: 16

'Forgive me Lord, I want to live my life for You alone'.
I am saved, born again.

LOVED

Declarations

1 John 4: 18 There is no fear in love; but perfect love casts out fear, because fear involves torment. But he who fears has not been made perfect in love.
I am loved perfectly
(I know every detail; your strengths, weaknesses, the past, the future. Trust Me: ; I want to bless you).

Rom 8: 15 For you did not receive the spirit of bondage again to fear, but you received the Spirit of adoption by whom we cry out 'Abba Father.'
I am loved intimately – 'abba' Father
(The veil is torn, be so open with Me, trust, delight in My embrace).

Is 54: 5 For your Maker is your husband, the Lord of hosts is His name; and your Redeemer is the Holy One of Israel; He is called the God of the whole earth.
– as by a perfect husband
(As the closest love relationship, as 'one'. Let it be, 'we' doing..............)

S of S 8: 6–7 Set me as a seal upon your heart, for love is as strong as death, jealousy as cruel as the grave; its flames are flames of fire a most vehement flame. Many waters cannot quench love, nor can the floods drown it. If a man would give for love all the wealth of his house, it would be utterly despised.
I am loved passionately as with the very flame of the Lord
(Nothing reserved or held back).

Rom 8: 39 nor height nor depth, nor any other created thing, shall be able to separate us from the love of God which is in Christ Jesus our Lord.
I cannot be separated from Your love

(Whatever the circumstances – no mountain too high or valley too low, I am there with you).

Eph 1: 4　　just as He chose us in Him before the foundation of the world, that we should be holy and without blame before Him in love.
I was chosen before the foundation of the world
(**You are unique. I have a special glorious purpose already planned for you**).

THE OLD HAS GONE

Declarations

Rom 6: 6　　knowing this, that our old man was crucified with Him, that the body of sin might be done away with...

2 Cor 5: 17　Therefore, if anyone is in Christ, he is a new creation; old things have passed away; behold, all things have become new.

Gal 2: 20　　I have been crucified with Christ; it is no longer I who live, but Christ lives in me; and the life which I now live in the flesh I live by faith in the Son of God who loved me and gave Himself for me.
I(old self centered 'I')**have been crucified with Christ**
(**The person you used to be is no more, that old self-centered independent person full of fear, pride, was buried with Me. When I rose from the dead, so did you as a new creation, a new person**).

Is 43: 1　　But now, thus says the Lord, who created you, O Jacob, and He who formed you, O Israel: 'Fear not, for I have redeemed you; I have called you by your name; you are Mine.

Eph 1: 7　　In Him we have redemption through His blood, the forgiveness of sins, according to the riches of His grace
I (new 'I') **have been redeemed through Your blood**
(**It is a perfect redemption. You are free from all the bondages of the curse – fear, oppression, negatives**).

Col 1: 13   He has delivered us from the power of darkness and con-
veyed us into the kingdom of the Son of His love,
I have been delivered from the power of darkness
(As if you no longer lived in the same country; now you
are in a new country, new language, new joys).

2 Tim 1: 7   For God has not given us a spirit of fear, but of power and
of love and of a sound mind.

1 John 4: 18 There is no fear in love; but perfect love casts our fear,
because fear involves torment. But he who fears has not
been made perfect in love.
I do not fear
(You are free from the fear of man and the need to worry.
My perfect love and power has replaced it. Your security
is now in Me, so in its place, delight in an awesome fear
of Me).

Rom 6: 14   For sin shall not have dominion over you, for you are not
under law but under grace.

Rom 8: 2   For the law of the Spirit of life in Christ Jesus has made
me free from the law of sin and death.
I am not under the law but under grace
(The weight of striving to please Me, of failure and suc-
cess, is now replaced by a delight in doing it for Me.)

Is 53: 4–5   Surely He has borne our sicknesses and carried our pains;
yet we esteemed Him stricken, smitten by God, and
afflicted. But He was wounded for our transgressions, He
was bruised for our iniquities; the chastisement for our
peace was upon Him, and by His stripes we are healed.

1 Pet 2: 24 who Himself bore our sins in is own body on the tree,
that we, having died to sins, might live for righteousness
– by whose stripes you were healed.
I have been healed
(The body that used to be sick is no more. Now you have
the same divine nature that I have. As I was when on
earth, you too are free from sickness, depression, confu-
sion, the past etc).

Gal 5: 1   Stand fast therefore in the liberty by which Christ has made us free, and do not be entangled again with a yoke of bondage.

I am free from every bondage
(I shed My blood because I love you, to cut you loose-from your culture, sin, yourself etc; so you are free to know Me).

Rom 8: 1   There is therefore now no condemnation to those who are in Christ Jesus, who do not walk according to the flesh, but according to the Spirit.

I am free from condemnation
(Know that that nagging accusation is from the enemy and give it no place).

MY NEW SELF

Gen 12: 2   I will make you a great nation; I will bless you and make your name great; and you shall be a blessing.

Eph 1: 3   Blessed be the God and Father of our Lord Jesus Christ, who has blessed us with every spiritual blessing in the heavenly places in Christ.

I am a blessing
(Your new nature has been so mightily blessed with every spiritual blessing. Let them flow naturally from you).

Eph 2: 8   For by grace you have been saved through faith, and that not of yourselves, it is the gift of God.

I live in grace
(Our life is a love relationship; such joy in your heart because you know that My grace will enable you to do whatever I ask of you).

1 Pet 1: 23   having been born again, not of corruptible seed but incorruptible, through the word of God which lives and abides forever.

Rom 8: 11   But if the Spirit of Him who raised Jesus from the dead dwells in you, He who raised Christ from the dead will also give life to your mortal bodies through His Spirit who dwells in you.

I have been born again through the divine incorruptible seed of the word of God

(Your whole being, including your mortal body throbs with My life).

2 Cor 5: 17 Therefore, if anyone is in Christ, he is a new creation; old things have passed away; behold, all things have become new.

I am a new creation

(You are a new species, no longer ordinary, My child; a new power source is flowing through you).

Eph 2: 10 For we are His workmanship, created in Christ Jesus for good works, which God prepared beforehand that we should walk in them.

I am Your workmanship

(My work of art; every day as you respond to Me saying, 'Yes Lord', I transform you to become more and more beautiful).

1 Cor 1: 30–31 But of Him you are in Christ Jesus, who became for us wisdom from God – and righteousness and sanctification and redemption – that, as it is written, 'He who glories, let him glory in the Lord'.

I am in Christ

(Hidden in Me, part of Me, My body).

Col 1: 27 To them God willed to make known what are the riches of the glory of this mystery among the Gentiles: which is Christ in you, the hope of glory.

and **Christ lives in me**

(All that I am, the fullness of God, lives, throbs in you).

John 15: 5 I am the vine, you are the branches. He who abides in Me, and I in him, bears much fruit; for without Me you can do nothing.

1 Thes 5: 17 pray without ceasing

I am one with you as a branch is of a vine; we

13

commune always

(No more do you yearn to get into My presence. You are there. We are one. There is no reason to leave My presence. Let My life flow through you, and bear much fruit).

Rom 5: 17   For if by the one man's offence death reigned through the one, much more those who receive abundance of grace and of the gift of righteousness will reign in life through the One, Jesus Christ.

I have received the gift of Your righteousness

(My nature, not through anything you do, but because of My shed blood. It is a love gift. Now, you are in My Presence with no sense of condemnation or inferiority, and you have the same authority over the enemy which I exercised. We are as one. My nature is in you, so, for example, no more do you try to love; you can 'be' love).

Prov 28: 1   The wicked flee when no one pursues, but the righteous are bold as a lion.

– so I am as bold as a lion

(Relying on Me within, you know no fear; expect only victory).

2 Pet 1: 3–4   ...His divine power has given to us all things that pertain to life and godliness, through the knowledge of Him who called us by glory and virtue, by which have been given to us exceedingly great and precious promises, that through these you may be partakers of the divine nature, having escaped the corruption that is in the world through lust.

I am a partaker of Your divine nature

(My life, the Word is living in you, is you. Like Me, you do not fear, you do not get sick; it is not your nature).

Rom 8: 15–17   For you did not receive the spirit of bondage again to fear, but you received the Spirit of adoption by whom we cry out, 'Abba, Father'. The Spirit Himself bears witness with our spirit that we are children of God, and if children, then heirs – heirs of God and joint heirs with Christ, ...

I am a son/daughter of the King of Kings

(A joint heir with Me, walk as royalty).

14

Phil 4: 19   And my God shall supply all your need according to His riches in glory by Christ Jesus.
I know You will supply all my needs
(The whole world is Mine. Even in the natural a father tries to supply the needs of his children. Much more will I provide for you my beloved).

John 17: 22   And the glory which You gave Me I have given them, that they may be one just as We are one;
Ps 97: 5   The mountains melt like wax at the presence of the Lord, at the presence of the Lord of the whole earth.
2 Cor 3: 18   But we all, with unveiled face, beholding as in a mirror the glory of the Lord, are being transformed into the same image from glory to glory, just as by the Spirit of the Lord.
I have received Your glory
(So that we can be as one, as I was with My Father. You carry My awesome Presence. My glory is more powerful than any cultural bondage. Mountains melt like wax in the Presence of the Lord. As you focus on Me, I change you from glory to glory).

2 Cor 1: 21   Now He who establishes us with you in Christ and has anointed us is God,
1 John   But the anointing which you have received from Him
2: 27   abides in you, and you do not need that anyone teach you; but as the same anointing teaches you concerning all things, and is true, and is not a lie, and just as it has taught you, you will abide in Him.
I am as anointed as You were when on earth
(Exactly the same source of super-natural power, the Holy Spirit, Who lived in Me is now in you. You can be as sensitive to My prompting as I was to My Father, and release whatever is required, as I did.)

1 Cor 2: 16   'For who has known the mind of the Lord that he may instruct Him?' But we have the mind of Christ.
I have Your mind, the mind of Christ
(Transformed by the living word. That old mindset,

self-centered, fearful and negative is becoming vibrant, positive and creative).

John 16: 13	However, when He, the Spirit of truth, has come, He will guide you into all truth; for He will not speak on His own authority, but whatever He hears He will speak; and He will tell you things to come.
1 Cor 2: 12	Now we have received, not the spirit of the world, but the Spirit who is from God, that we might know the things that have been freely given to us by God. **I am able to understand the Truth and mysteries** **(Delight in the truth, be so expectant and I will reveal My heart to you).**
John 10: 27	My sheep hear My voice, and I know them, and they follow Me. **I hear Your voice** **(Expect Me to guide, prompt, even speak to you twenty four hours a day, whatever you are doing).**
Is 12: 2–3	Behold, God is my salvation, I will trust and not be afraid; 'For Yah, the Lord, is my strength and song; He also has become my salvation.' Therefore with joy you will draw water from the wells of salvation.
John 4: 14	… But the water that I shall give him will become in him a fountain of water springing up into everlasting life.
John 7: 38	He who believes in Me, as the Scripture has said, out of his heart will flow rivers of living water. **I draw water with joy from the well of salvation within** **(All of Me, My love, joy, peace, wisdom, power, healing, forgiveness etc, is within you. Continually draw from it with joy, with confidence, and release it.)**
Rom 12: 3	For I say, through the grace given to me, to everyone who is among you, not to think of himself more highly than he ought to think, but to think soberly, as God has dealt to each one a measure of faith.

Rom 1: 17   For in it (the gospel) the righteousness of God is revealed from faith to faith; as it is written, 'The just shall live by faith'.
I have Your faith within
(a divinely implanted measure of faith – use it so that it grows from faith to faith).

1 Cor 1: 30   But of Him you are in Christ Jesus, who became for us wisdom from God – and righteousness and sanctification and redemption –
I have Your wisdom within
(Expect it to flow when you draw it up from the well within).

Rom 5: 5   Now hope does not disappoint, because the love of God has been poured out in our hearts by the Holy Spirit who was given to us.
I have Your love within
(Including My zeal. It compels you be that chosen vessel through whom My glorious purposes are realized. I implore you to release it to bless this hungry desolate world).

John 14: 27   Peace I leave with you, My peace I give to you; not as the world gives do I give to you. Let not your heart be troubled, neither let it be afraid.
I have Your peace within
(Such confidence in Me, wholeness, rest).

John 15: 11   These things I have spoken to you, that My joy may remain in you, and that your joy may be full.
Neh 8: 10   .....Do not sorrow, for the joy of the Lord is your strength.
I have Your joy within
(The fruit of being one with Me as two lovers and it is your strength in any circumstance).

Prov 29: 18   Where there is no revelation (prophetic vision), the peo-

ple cast off restraint; but happy is he who keeps the law.
I have a vision
**(Let it be a driving force, to walk just as I walked, with
all the supernatural gifts flowing. Seek Me re your indi-
vidual vision and then ardently pursue it. Keep it burning,
do not let the enemy quench it).**

AUTHORITY

Col 2: 15   Having disarmed principalities and powers, He made a
public spectacle of them, triumphing over them in it.
**I know You have defeated the enemy; You triumphed
over him**
**(Now you are in Me, so make the decision never to be
defeated by him).**

Luke 10: 19 Behold I give **you** the authority to trample on serpents
and scorpions, and over all the power of the enemy, and
nothing shall by any means hurt you.
**I have been given this authority to trample on serpents
and scorpions and over all the power of the enemy**
**(re all aspects of the curse – sickness, depression, fear etc:
Walk in this authority purchased for you. He is under
your feet. Whatever form he tries to take, decide he will
become as dust. Do not just be defensive. What are you
going to tread on today?)**

James 4: 7   Therefore submit to God. Resist the devil and he will flee
from you.
I resist the devil and he has to flee
**(He is as terrified of you as he was of Me when you stand
in and use that authority).**

Phil 2: 9–10 Therefore God also has highly exalted Him and given
Him the name which is above every name, that at the
name of Jesus every knee should bow, of those in heaven,
and of those on earth, and of those under the earth,

I use the Name of Jesus knowing every knee must
bow to the King of Kings
(– it is as if I am speaking).

Mark 11: 23 For assuredly, I say to you, whoever says to this mountain, 'Be removed and be cast into the sea, ' and does not
doubt in his heart, but believes that those things he says
will be done, he will have whatever he says.
**I speak to mountains (problems) and they are removed
(Know the authority in your mouth; nothing is impossible for you).**

1 John 5: 4 For whatever is born of God overcomes the world. And
this is the victory that has overcome the world – our faith.
2 Cor 2: 14 Now thanks be to God who always leads us in triumph
in Christ, and through us diffuses the fragrance of His
knowledge in every place.
Heb 3: 6 ...And it is we who are [now members] of this house, if
we hold fast and firm to the end our joyful and exultant
confidence and sense of triumph in our hope [in Christ]
(Amplified Bible).
**I am an overcomer; victory is certain – with joy I
hold fast to Your Word
(Fight the fight of faith, refuse to accept defeat).**

Rom 8: 37 Yet in all these things we are more than conquerors
through Him who loved us.
**I am more than a conqueror
(Not just a conqueror; the issue is what to do with the
spoils).**

Rom 5: 17 For if by one man's offence death reigned through the
one, much more those who receive abundance of grace
and of the gift of righteousness will reign in life through
the One, Jesus Christ.
Math 10: 8 Heal the sick, cleanse the lepers, raise the dead, cast out
demons. Freely you have received, freely give.
**I reign as a king in life
(Rule, speak to your body, relationships and circumstances,**

destroy the works of the enemy, release the kingdom of God).

Eph 6: 11   Put on the whole armour of God, that you may be able to stand against the wiles of the devil.
I wear and use the armour of God
(Stand in the fullness of what I have given you and refuse to be moved).

Deut 28: 13 And the Lord will make you the head and not the tail; you shall be above only, and not beneath, if you heed the commandments of the Lord your God....
1 John 4: 4 You are of God, little children, and have overcome them, because He who is in you is greater than he who is in the world.
I am the head and not the tail
(The strongest spirit dominates, and greater is He that is in you, than he that is in the world. Do not tolerate any work of the enemy).

Eph 4:   'Be angry, and do not sin': do not let the sun go down
26–27   on your wrath, nor give place to the devil.
Rom 12: 9 Let love be without hypocrisy. Abhor what is evil. Cling to what is good.
I am angry at what the enemy has done, hate what is evil, and refuse to be lulled to sleep and compromise
(Let My love in you stir up righteous anger instilling a passion to release those in bondage).

James 1: 2–4 My brethren, count it all joy when you fall into various trials, knowing that the testing of your faith produces patience. But let patience have its perfect work, that you may be perfect and complete, lacking nothing.
Acts 4:   'Now, Lord, look on their threats, and grant to Your ser-
29–30   vants that with all boldness they may speak Your word, by stretching out Your hand to heal, and that signs and wonders may be done through the name of Your holy Servant Jesus'.

I see trials as new challenges, and rejoice in them
(You know I will intervene gloriously).

WALK

Deut 6: 5 You shall love the Lord your God with all your heart, with all your soul, and with all your strength.

Math 22: 37 Jesus said to him, 'You shall love the Lord your God with all your heart, with all your soul, and with all your mind'.
I love You with all my heart, all my soul and all my strength
(nothing left over).

1 Pet 1: 8–9 whom having not seen you love. Though now you do not see Him, yet believing, you rejoice with joy inexpressible and full of glory, receiving the end of your faith – the salvation of your souls.
I love You so I am filled with an inexpressible, triumphant and heavenly joy
(Involves your mind, will, emotions, body so this is total salvation, nothing left out – I love it).

Rom 5: 5 Now hope does not disappoint, because the love of God has been poured out in our hearts by the Holy Spirit who was given to us.

Eph 3: 19 to know the love of Christ which passes knowledge; that you may be filled with all the fullness of God.
I am getting to know Your love for me and experiencing being filled with all Your fullness
(If not living in My fullness, there is more to know....)

Ps 40: 8 'I delight to do Your will, O my God, and Your law is withln my heart'.
I delight to do Your will,

1 Thess Rejoice always.
5: 16 **– rejoicing always**

Jer 31: 33   But this is the covenant that I will make with the house of Israel after those days, says the Lord; I will put My law in their minds, and write it on their hearts; and I will be their God, and they shall be My people.

Rom 8: 2   For the law of the Spirit of life in Christ Jesus has made me free from the law of sin and death.

Phil 2: 12–13   .....work out your own salvation with fear and trembling; for it is God who works in you both to will and to do for His good pleasure.

I delight in Your laws that are in my heart.
(They are part of me and work in me to love and to walk with Your faith – hallelujah!

Matt 22: 39   And the second (great commandment) is like it; 'You shall love your neighbor as yourself'.

I love others with the same(passionate)love,

Math 6: 15   But if you do not forgive men their trespasses, neither will your Father forgive your trespasses.

– and am quick to forgive
(To restore love).

1 John 4: 4   You are of God, little children, and have overcome them, because He who is in you is greater than he who is in the world.

I walk in the power of Your love
(My love in you is greater, above the self-centredness in the world)

Rom 12: 11   Never lag in zeal and in earnest endeavour; be aglow and burning with the Spirit, serving the Lord (Amplified Bible).

I am aglow, burning in the spirit serving You
(With joy and zeal).

Prov 4: 23   Keep your heart with all diligence, for out of it spring the issues of life.

I keep my heart with all diligence
(Not to grieve Me; no trace of pride or self-thoughts).

Gal 5: 16   I say then: Walk in the Spirit, and you shall not fulfil the lust of the flesh.

I walk in the Spirit,

Rom 8: 14   For as many as are led by the Spirit of God, these are sons of God.

– am led by the Spirit

Eph 5: 18   And do not be drunk with wine, in which is dissipation; but be filled with the Spirit

– and filled with the Spirit

(In harmony with Me, 100% submitted; always expectant of Me).

2 Cor 4: 18   while we do not look at the things which are seen, but at the things which are not seen. For the things which are seen are temporary, but the things which are not seen are eternal.

Rom 8: 5–6   For those who live according to the flesh set their minds on the things of the flesh, but those who live according to the Spirit, the things of the Spirit. For to be carnally minded is death, but to be spiritually minded is life and peace.

I focus on things unseen; my mind is set on things of the Spirit

(My glorious purposes. The effect is life and peace).

1 Sam 16: 7   But the Lord said to Samuel, 'Do not look at his appearance or at his physical stature, because I have refused him. For the Lord does not see as man sees; for man looks at the outward appearance, but the Lord looks at the heart.'

2 Cor 5: 16   Therefore, from now on, we regard no one according to the flesh. Even though we have known Christ according to the flesh, yet now we know Him thus no longer.

I do not respond to the appearance of others, but their hearts

(their relationship with Me and how to encourage them).

John 4: 24   God is Spirit, and those who worship Him must worship in spirit and truth.

I worship in spirit and truth

(Draw with joy from the spirit within. It is the love language of your heart: it can be expressed in so many ways. With all your heart soul and body embrace Me and the Word, so there is harmony in you, no hypocrisy. It will be as an open heaven; like an electric circuit open to the source of your life).

1 Thes 5: 17 pray without ceasing
– praying always
(Switched on continually, whatever you are doing).

Phil 4: 13   I can do all things through Christ who strengthens me.
I know that I can do all things You ask of me through the anointing within
(No limit – All of My glorious power will flow as required).

Prov 3: 5   Trust in the Lord with all your heart, and lean not on your own understanding;
I trust You with all my heart
(You rely on Me, you know I am faithful).

John 1: 1, 14   In the beginning was the Word, and the Word was with God, and the Word was God. And the Word became flesh and dwelt among us, and we beheld His glory, the glory as of the only begotten of the Father, full of grace and truth.
I trust the Word, the Truth, as You are the Word
(rest your weight on it).

Is: 66: 2   '… But on this one will I look; on him who is poor and of a contrite spirit, and who trembles at My word'.
I tremble at Your word
(your heart saying, 'Yes Lord'. It reveals My awesome glorious power – receive it by faith and do it).

Jer 15: 16   Your words were found, and I ate them, and Your word was to me the joy and rejoicing of my heart;
I feast on the Word; it is the joy and rejoicing of my heart

(Embrace it, eat it, and digest it, so that it ignites within).

Heb 4: 12   For the word of God is living and powerful, and sharper than any two-edged sword, piercing even to the division of soul and spirit, and of joints and marrow, and is a discerner of the thoughts and intents of the heart.

**– it is living and powerful, sharper than any
two-edged sword**
**(It penetrates the depths of your heart, able to change
you, release you – Glory to God!).**

1 Thes 2: 13 ....the word of God which you heard from us, you welcomed it not as the word of men, but as it is in truth, the word of God, which also effectively words in you who believe.

– it is working effectively in me
(Expect miracles daily).

Rom 4:
20–21   He did not waver at the promise of God through unbelief, but was strengthened in faith, giving glory to God, and being fully convinced that what He had promised He was also able to perform.

**I do not stagger at Your promise but embrace it with
joy**
**(Know that I long for you to receive it. This is the fight of
faith, through which you will grow strong).**

Mark 11: 24 Therefore I say to you, whatever things you ask when you pray, believe that you receive them, and you will have them.

I pray, speak out the Word and receive it now
**(Even if not evident, possess it, be pregnant with it;
declare it done, give thanks for it).**

Prov 18: 21 Death and life are in the power of the tongue, and those who love it will eat its fruit.

I know life and death are in the power of my tongue
**(Only speak out good positive words, and they will come
into being. Never speak negatively).**

1 Thes 5: 18 in everything give thanks: for this is the will of God in Christ Jesus for you.
I give thanks in everything
(For My presence with you, and in trials for the outcome which you speak into being).

2 Cor 5: 7 For we walk by faith, not by sight,

Heb 11: 6 But without faith it is impossible to please Him, for he who comes to God must believe that He is, and that He is a rewarder of those who diligently seek Him.

1 Pet 1: 7 .... the genuineness of your faith, being much more precious than gold that perishes, though it is tested by fire, may be found to praise, honor, and glory at the revelation of Jesus Christ,
I walk by faith, not by sight
(Stand on the promise, not affected by circumstances or feelings).

Heb 4: For we who have believed do enter that rest, ...

3, 10 For he who has entered His rest has himself also ceased from his works as God did from His.
I believe, so I have entered Your rest and ceased from struggling
(Now, your confidence is in Me; you rely on Me, on the Word. Your life is becoming a manifestation of the Word).

Gal 6: 14 But God forbid that I should boast except in the cross of our Lord Jesus Christ, by whom the world has been crucified to me, and I to the world.
I glory, even boast in the power of the cross and the power of Your blood
(Look at what I and your Father have done for you – the glorious abundant life now yours).

John 15: 5 I am the vine, you are the branches. He who abides in Me, and I in him, bears much fruit; for without Me you can do nothing.
I abide in You, Your word, so I produce much fruit
(fruit that remains).

1 John 2: 6   He who says he abides in Him ought himself also to walk just as He walked.
         – and walk just as You did,

Mk 16:
17–18   And these signs will follow those who believe; In My name they will cast out demons; they will speak with new tongues; they will take up serpents; and if they drink anything deadly, it will by no means hurt them; they will lay hands on the sick, and they will recover.
         – laying hands on the sick and seeing them recover
         (through touch, releasing My Spirit to evict the spirit that sustains the sickness).

John 7: 38   'He who believes in Me, as the Scripture has said, out of his heart will flow rivers of living water.'

Is 11: 2–3   The Spirit of the Lord shall rest upon Him, the Spirit of wisdom and understanding, the Spirit of counsel and might, the Spirit of knowledge and of the fear of the Lord. His delight is in the fear of the Lord.....
I release continually rivers of living water
(drawing from the well of salvation, the fullness of Your spirit and Your life).

Ezek 47: 9   And it shall be that every living thing that moves, wherever the rivers go, will live. There will be a very great multitude of fish, because these waters go there; for they will be healed, and everything will live wherever the river goes.
         ...bringing life wherever I go
         (My love flowing from you, melting hearts, and just as I did opening eyes, releasing captives).

PURPOSE

Exod 19:
5–6   Now therefore, if you will indeed obey My voice and keep My covenant, then you shall be a special treasure to Me above all people; for all the earth is Mine, and you shall be to Me a kingdom of priests and a holy nation'....

1 Pet 2: 9   But you are a chosen generation, a royal priesthood, a

holy nation, His own special people, that you may proclaim the praises of Him who called you out of darkness into His marvelous light;
For You to be glorified
(In everything you think, speak and do – open heaven).

Math 6: 10 Your kingdom come, Your will be done on earth as it is in heaven.
To establish Your kingdom on earth
(All knowing Me, the Word, and living it).

1 John 3: 8 ...For this purpose the Son of God was manifested, that He might destroy the works of the devil.
To destroy the works of the enemy
(That have tied up so many).

Luke 4: 18 The Spirit of the Lord is upon Me, because has anointed Me to preach the gospel to the poor; He has sent Me to heal the brokenhearted, to proclaim liberty to the captives and recovery of sight to the blind, to set at liberty those who are oppressed;
Mark 16: 20 And they went out and preached everywhere, the Lord working with them and confirming the word through the accompanying signs. Amen.
To preach the gospel
(expecting miracles to confirm the Word),
To release captives, open blind eyes and heal the broken hearted
(Expect divine encounters).

John 17: 18 Just as You sent Me into the world, I also have sent them into the world (Amplified Bible).
To walk as You did when on earth, revealing Your glory
(Walking on water, with no props – manifesting the same God given love and authority; doing the same glorious things).

HOW TO LIVE A SCRIPTURE

The Word of God is BRILLIANT

It is glorious to have the **Living Word** inside us, to know the truth of the Word deep within. Then when we speak the Word, the situation is changed, the person is healed, we find the job, relationships are restored etc:

'Is not My Word like a fire?' says the Lord, 'and like a hammer that breaks in pieces the rock (of most stubborn resistance)?' Jer 23: 29 (Amplified Bible).

What joy it is to step into the Word, to possess it, to live it. In Luke 4: 21 Jesus announced that **'Today this Scripture is fulfilled in your hearing'**. Jesus stepped into that scripture. In other words, He said 'This Scripture describes Me'. We can similarly make any scripture our possession; especially those describing who we are as new creations or ones that have particularly touched our heart.

I have made use of the word **'BRILLIANT'** to help us to digest a specific scripture and live it out. The **Word** is **Brilliant** in what it can do in and through us. The consonants in **'BRILLIANT'** can be used to provide a structure for this.

BELIEVE	Know it is the living Word, spoken by Almighty God
RECEIVE	Possess it personally with joy
LIVE IT evident in	Language – speak it out
LIVE IT evident in	Lifestyle – changing the way you behave
NOW	Today release it, use it
TRIUMPHANTLY	Know it works

How does it work?

Take a scripture, one that has spoken to you, or perhaps one of the Declarations in 'JUST LIVE IT'. Then use it as follows;

BELIEVE	Know it is the living Word, spoken by Almighty God. Tremble at His word. Thank Him for the truth.

Believe as a child believes.
Lay aside the old negative thinking of the world.
Let Him speak to you as if He is in the room
with you.

RECEIVE

Possess it with **Joy** personally, with a **thankful
heart**.
Put your name in the scripture.
Again give no place to your old way of thinking.
Receive it deep inside with such joy.
Delight in it – meditate on it.
Speak it out often, softly, loudly.
Know as you do, as you say the same as the
Scriptures, you will become more and more
confident and excited about it.
A young child given a strange present, may look
at it from different angles, touch it, explore it. All
his attention is focused on it, so he gets to
know it, even before using it.
You can similarly explore and delight in the truth.
Use your mind to the full; what does this word
mean?
Are there any other similar scriptures?
The Holy Spirit Who lives in you will help to
reveal the
glory of the truth.

LIVE IT evident in my   **Language** –
Decide, I will delight in speaking out this truth,
sharing with others its beauty, excitement...

LIVE IT evident in my   **Lifestyle** –
Decide to put it to work. I will no longer react as
I always have done.
I now **know** the truth so there will be **victory** in
this area.

NOW

Today my life will be different. Think of specific
times or places, or issues, which will not be the
same – Hallelujah!

TRIUMPHANTLY Know it will happen.

Be so **expectant** that the Holy Spirit, who is living in you, will move mightily in you to see that it happens – that it will be a reality today.

Example

'There is no fear in love; but perfect love casts out fear, because fear involves torment. He who fears has not been made perfect in love.' (1 John 4: 18).

'I am loved perfectly'

Believe

It is so glorious, that I am loved perfectly by Almighty God. As I get to **know** this truth **inside,** I will be free of fear, of people, circumstances etc: – praise God!

The Scriptures show His love. It is there throughout the Old Testament. His people rebelled again and again, but God longed for them to return to Him so He could bless them. **'I will heal their back-sliding, I will love them freely, for my anger has turned away from him (Israel)'** (Hos14: 4). This perfect love is shown in the Gospels. How He sent His precious Son to die, so that all of us who have gone our own way could know Him, and receive the extraordinary inheritance He has won for us. Almighty God had, and always has had, wonderful plans for His own children. That means for me. These plans can only be mine if I believe and respond to this beautiful love. **I will believe it!**

Thank You Lord for this truth. It is the **living Word of Almighty God**. I tremble at Your Word; I dare not disagree with any part of it. I will give no place to my old 'caterpillar' mind, full of negatives, and fear. I will believe Your truth as a child believes – and trusts. I will believe it as if You were standing in the room speaking to me – Thank You Lord.

Receive

With **joy** and such a thankful heart I receive this love. I believe what Your Word says, that **God Almighty loves me (my name)**, that **I am so precious to Him**. Thank You Lord. Let joy rise up from within. What peace and confidence it gives me.

I will delight in Your love and think much about what it means for me. I am loved perfectly. I will speak it often, softly – whisper it so it sinks deep into my heart. You are with me always, I can never be alone. Nothing can separate me from Your love. I have been through tough times, but You were with me, You brought me through. You know every detail about my life, my strengths and weaknesses, successes and failures, and yet You still love me. Even more glorious is that You want to bless me. I will speak it loudly, declaring it, or even sing it – You have glorious plans for me – wow!

How can I fear when I know You love me perfectly and You are with me always? I will totally trust in this glorious truth.

Live it – Language

I will not keep to myself how wonderful it is to know that I am loved by You. I may even sing about You – not just when alone! I will encourage others to know this beautiful love for themselves – hallelujah

Live it – Lifestyle

I will not hide this joy in my heart. I will have a new twinkle in my eye. I will be ready to share about why I have this inner joy and confidence with anyone I meet.

I have been frightened of my (husband, boss, child, work etc,) but not now. When I see them there will be such peace in my heart, such confidence in You. I will be able to love them with Your love. I know You will give me the words to say – praise God!

Now

Today I will be different, when by myself, on the way to work, while working, in the shops, wherever I am there will be a new joy in my heart. I refuse to fear. …Instead, I expect You to protect me, to give me wisdom or whatever I need.

Triumphantly

I know it will work. I am so expectant. I know others will see a difference in me and be drawn to You as a result – praise God!

I will no longer be the victim, but will shine with Your love, Your life. The situation will be changed – glory to God!